I Can Pray to God

written by Sandra Brooks

illustrated by Gwen Connelly

Third Edition, 1994
Library of Congress Catalog Card No. 88-63575
© 1989, The Standard Publishing Company, Cincinnati, Ohio
A di· ision of Standex International Corporation. Printed in U.S.A.

Guess what, God?
I learned something new today!

I learned that You made
the big, wide world
and the big, blue sky
and the deep, blue sea
and everything in them.

You even made me!

Guess what else I learned today, God?

I learned that You made every person different and special, and no one is exactly like me. Do You know how I know that, God?

Mommy told me. She told me when
we had our play time this morning.

"I have a surprise for you," she said.
"We're going to do something new
today. Something that's very special
and lots and lots of fun."

First Mommy showed me how to mix plaster. Next she let me pour it into a pan. Then Mommy took my hand and put it on top of the plaster. She pressed on my hand and then carefully lifted it up.

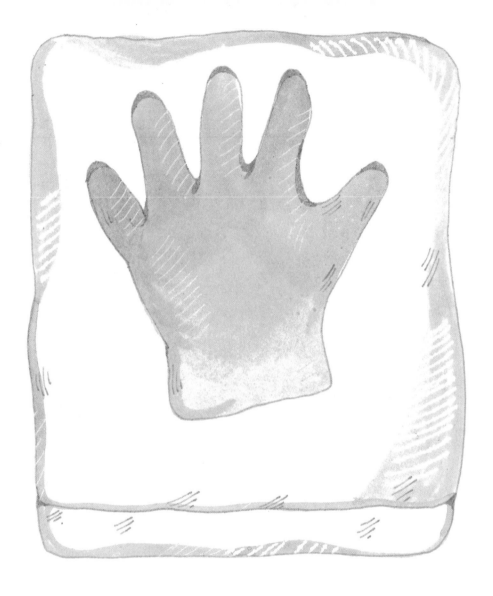

There it was! My handprint.

"Look at how the plaster shows the lines on your fingertips," Mommy said. "No one has fingerprints exactly like yours. God gave everyone a different set of fingerprints."

"Imagine that!" I said. "I have my very own set of fingerprints!"

Mommy wrote my name and the date in the plaster.

"When you grow up," she said, "you'll be able to see how small your hand used to be."

Then she told me the best part of all.
She said my hands are small, but I
can still do important things. I can
pray, and when I do, it's like placing
my hand in Yours, God. That means I
can do things that are just as
important as the things that grown-ups
do.

She showed me how to use the
fingers on my hand to help me pray.

She said my thumb is closest to my
heart. It can remind me to pray for
everyone I love most—like Mommy and
Daddy and my relatives and friends.

My preacher and my teachers sometimes use their index fingers to point out lessons in the Bible or my schoolwork. That reminds me to pray for my preacher and the teachers in my church and in my school.

My middle finger stands high above all the other fingers on my hand. It reminds me to pray for our president and other leaders in our government.

My ring finger is the weakest finger
on my hand. It reminds me to pray for
people who are sick or unhappy.

The last finger on my hand is smallest. It reminds me to pray for myself. By praying for myself last, I learn to think of what other people need as well as what I need.

I learn to do as Jesus said. He said that I should love my neighbor as myself. My neighbor is anyone I know about. So I should love and pray for anyone I know about.

Just one more thing before I go, God.

Thank You for making
the big, wide world
and the big, blue sky
and the deep, blue sea
and everything in them.

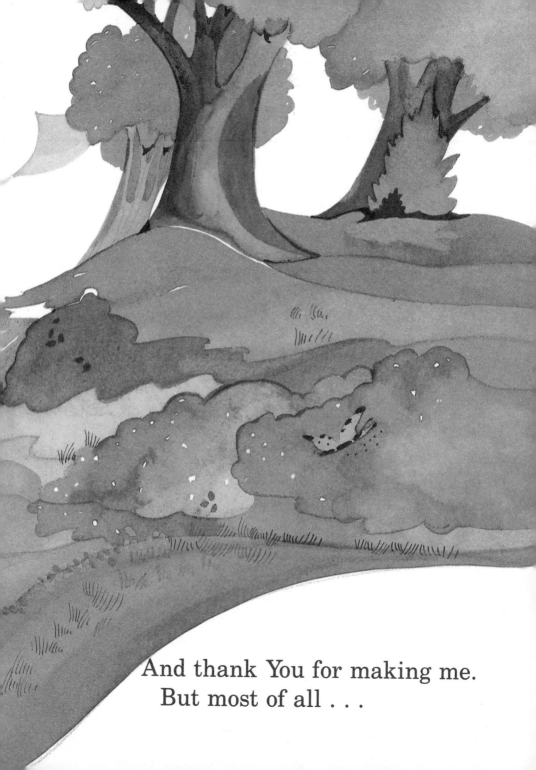

And thank You for making me.
But most of all . . .

... thank You for loving me. Thank You for taking my hand in Yours and making me able to do something just as important as any grown-up can do. 'Cause that's what happens ...

... when I pray.